aliza grace

moving on will taste bitter

until its six months from now

and you forget

how it felt

the moment he saw you

for you

aliza grace

you can stop watering dead plants

aliza grace

the ugly truth

there is no

right person

wrong time

he loves you

but he wont change

he misses you

and never shows up

sometimes you will feel the weight of the
world on your shoulders
that is ok
-you are human

know that you are worth more

look at what you are giving

-the bare minimum

things I am not ready for:

unsharring our location

changing your name in my phone

no more pinky promises

telling my family

-becoming strangers

teach me to be like you

so that I can forget

how you made me feel

all the love in the beginning

and the pain you left in the end

my trust is like a mirror

you can fix it

if it were to break

but

you will still see cracks in the reflection

somethings I will never understand

like how someone can spend so much time

growing loving learning together

and then break you

make you question everything

you have ever known

the worst feeling

that I have ever felt

was the morning

after we broke up

-*ifykyk*

humble yourself

and show your neighbor

the kindness

you wish you were shown

life is hard

you know

what you do now

will be a reflection of yourself

in the years to come

know that if you are in

the absolute worst place

of your life right now

it can only get better

aliza grace

my favorite color was black
until you were buried in it

the hardest thing that you have ever done

is walk away

while you are still madly in love

I am a strong believer

that you do not

fall out of love

and if you do

you were never really

in love

the words I wish I had said

you look me in the eyes

while I say them

because you loved brown eyes

they would tear up

as I pour my hurt out to you

by the time I finish

both of our souls emptied

out on the concrete driveway

we knew it could not be fixed

love exists im sure

because I see the way I love you

knowing a lot

takes time

not in the cliché way

you have to love and lose

build and break

we will never be those naive kids again

we have experienced the loss

of a lifetime

but only now

we can experience the love

of a lifetime

you cannot hurt the person you love

-it doesn't work that way

if you have to beg them

to love you

the way you love them

the best thing to do is leave

love yourself with the love you gave

so much

that they look back

and see you as their greatest loss

feeling smothered

when someone

asks you a question

you know the answer

but it just wont come out

-social anxiety

he never knew what he had

when he had it

until it was long gone

and he was left

with just the memory

it will be the middle of spring

when you get over me

you will look for me

in every girl after

searching

but you wont find me

because I cannot be replaced

you were a moment in life

-that ends too soon

allow yourself to feel

the raw emotions of a breakup

there is beauty in pain

after all

in a month

my skin will be replaced

with new skin

-your touch will be gone

loving you was giving everything

and getting nothing in return

-im moving on

people say

time heals

it is true

but they never

tell you

how much time

you will need

the missing

will end

you will move on

months from now

you will find the right

person

-*you wont look back*

the right guy will buy you flowers

without you having to ask

the kindest people are the most vulnerable

but they will not show you that side

until they can trust you

when that happens

you will feel their emotions

pouring out in your lap

-*you will know*

autumn is red

wears a satin dress

she is the nicest season

but autumn would never admit that

because her soul is made out of

the softest soil

her air is crisp

-when we fell in love

life is what you make of it

so live unapologetically

don't look back

yet

I thought brown eyes

wasn't that special

until I was lost in his

do not blame yourself

for other peoples choices

when you meet the one

you will know

you will be sure

because they feel like home

whenever I am old

looking back at life

I hope to have you

beside of me

-reliving

find comfort in the little things

getting to sleep in on a monday

the air on a rainy day

watching the sun set

take your dreams

run with them

life is short

so live

the sun will come out

in the morning

she will dance in the sky

because you are still learning

I honestly do not think I could love you more then I already do. and the fact that I can even wrap my head around that scares me. out of all the people in the world I choose you, and ill choose you for a lifetime...

-r

a hero would sacrifice you

to save the world

a villain would sacrifice the world

to save you

for all the girls

with boyfriends that

call you insecure

because your telling them

not to look at other women

leave

when you find someone

who respects your boundaries

you will not have to tell them twice

because they heard you the first time

thank you

I cried

for breaking up with me

how you did

if it had never happened that way

I would not be here

blooming

into the beam of light

I am today

aliza grace

time changes things

time heals

time takes you places

but most importantly

time teaches will bring us together

in the end

I don't know what I missed more

was it the way you didn't show up

or the fact you never called

how you made that face

when I caught you in your lies

maybe

I miss the person

I thought you were

moving on made me realize

that things remain the same

the sun will still rise in the morning

it will still set in the evening

you can

get through it

its okay to cry

remember the happiness you had

before them

thank them for the memories

do not dwell too long

-how to move on

nothing ever prepares you

for getting your heart broken

if he wants you

you will not have to question it

falling in love after getting your heart broken

you will learn how to trust

again

you will learn to love

again

everything works out in the end

and if it doesn't

then its not the end

aliza grace

goodbyes are always the hardest

he is not mine to love anymore

but you still do

more then she ever will

my love

cannot be replaced

you will search for me

in every girl

after me

aliza grace

maturing is when you

love the way you want to be loved

people say

some losses

set us free

this is true

love is like walking through a field of flowers

effortlessly beautiful

I see you different now

you are not the sweet boy

I fell in love with

what happened

It is so obvious

this missing you

catching myself thinking

about you

one time a day

because you never leave my mind

you can get through this

what you are going through right now

I believe in you

my love for you will last a lifetime

and longer

even if you decide

its not me anymore

pure love

I don't regret us anymore

I don't regret a single thing that happened

aliza grace

people change like seasons

your heart is golden

and kind

do not let anyone change that

aliza grace

I could fall in love with you

one thousand

times

for one thousand different reasons

aliza grace

author's note

firstly, I would like to thank you for giving my book
a chance, I greatly appreciate it.

secondly, the poems shared in this book are simply
about heartbreak, missing someone, or learning to
love again.

I hope these words resonate in some way.

god loves you

Printed in Great Britain
by Amazon